Wounded Knee
&
The Ghost Dance
Tragedy

MEMORIAL EDITION

Jack Utter

NATIONAL WOODLANDS PUBLISHING COMPANY

Lake Ann, Michigan

WOUNDED KNEE & THE GHOST DANCE TRAGEDY
(Memorial Edition)

Copyright © 1991 by National Woodlands Publishing Company

First Edition: April 1991

First Printing: April 1991
Second Printing: June 1991
Third Printing: April 1995

Publisher's Cataloging in Publication Data

Utter, Jack
    Wounded Knee & the Ghost Dance tragedy / Jack Utter
    29 p   23 cm
    Includes bibliographical references, 6 photos, 2 maps
    Preassigned LCCN: 91-61211
    ISBN 0-9628075-1-6
    1. Indians of North America – Sioux.   2. Indians of North America – Battles.   3. Wounded Knee (S.D.) – History.

95 96 97 98 99   10 9 8 7 6 5 4 3

C O N T E N T S

PREFACE

*H*ow long is 100 years ago? For many, especially in our future-oriented society, it is too far back to have much meaning. For others, it may seem barely behind yesterday.

There is a man in my small community who, early in the fall of 1990, got his picture in the local newspaper the week he became a centenarian. Almost every morning on a nationwide television program, birthday photographs of people the same age as this man, or up to a decade older, are aired. These people all have something in common with everyone at Wounded Knee. They were upon the earth at the same time…feeling the same sun, seeing the same moon, and breathing from the same reservoir of air. How long is 100 years ago? A little less than one full lifetime.

In American culture, as in many others, we make a point of celebrating the century marks of important events. The year 1989 was the bi-centennial for the U.S. Constitution. *That year also marked the centennial of the Sioux Land Cession of 1889, whereby "The Great Sioux Reservation," already reduced by 9,000,000 acres in 1876, was eliminated and carved up into six smaller reservations.*

In 1990-1991 the USDA Forest Service is sponsoring an important national celebration of the Forest Reserve Act of 1891, which initiated the national forest system and America's first continuing policy of conservation. *The 1890-1891 Ghost Dance Campaign and the Wounded Knee tragedy are being much more strongly remembered by the Sioux, part of whose very sacred Paha Sapa, or Black Hills, now constitute the Black Hills National Forest.*

In 1992, we will see a large national observance of the 500th anniversary of the landing of Columbus – an event marking the beginning of Euro-America. *For the Sioux and all other remaining Native American tribes, 1992 also marks the 500th anniversary of a beginning…of the end of their traditional cultures, or even their existence as tribes.*

Though the countless wrongs cannot be righted, it is appropriate for those of us who originated outside the Americas to keep in mind events that are important to the first Americans. Their general ancestors were the original possessors of all the land of our present nation, and some were watching from the beach as Columbus dropped anchor.

This booklet may best be described as a memorial piece. Simply stated, a memorial is a keepsake. There are two kinds: tangible, such as monuments, and intangible, which take their form in memories. Though the tangible form of this publication may pass away from the reader, I hope the memory will not.

Jack Utter
Prescott, Arizona
March 1991

INTRODUCTION

The tragedy at Wounded Knee was much more than a brief engagement between a band of Lakota and U.S. Army troops. Officially, it was the major battle in the Sioux Ghost Dance War of 1890-1891. In effect, Wounded Knee signified the end of a four-century armed struggle by Native Americans against multi-national, state-sponsored, and often violent oppression. The dream of freedom from Euro-American society was forever obliterated on a December day in 1890. The U.S. Census Report for the same year declared the ending of the American Frontier. Wounded Knee can be considered the capstone of that ending. A short summary follows, derived largely from Smith (1975), as well as Mooney (1896), and Capps (1975).

On the morning of December 29, 1890, the last significant armed conflict between the U.S. Army and the American Indian took place. The location was a campsite beside Wounded Knee Creek on the Pine Ridge Reservation in South Dakota. The government referred to the event as a battle, while the Sioux called it a massacre. It was almost entirely a massacre and only partly a battle, as very few of the Indians were armed or able to fight back in any way. Chief Big Foot and 370 of his followers were in the camp, under a flag of truce, having surrendered to the Seventh Cavalry the day before. Two-thirds of the Indians were women and children. The surrounding Army force consisted of 470 soldiers, including 32 Sioux scouts and a four-gun battery of light artillery. Fevered gunfire erupted, precipitated by fear, defiance, confusion, and blunder. By the time the smoke cleared, roughly 300 Indians lay dead – their bodies scattered across the cold ground. The federals lost 31 killed. Some of these deaths were caused by the crossfire of their own weapons.

Involved in the Wounded Knee tragedy, either centrally or peripherally, were a number of diverse personalities. There were the great Sioux Chiefs, Sitting Bull and Red Cloud. There was Wovoka, the Paiute Indian in Nevada who thought he was Christ returned to earth – and whose followers were certain he was. There was Buffalo Bill Cody, and there was General Nelson Miles who would, in years to come, command the U.S. Army in the Spanish-American War. Accompanying the General was Frederic Remington, the celebrated artist, who would publish famous and influential paintings of the "battle" (though he was not present) shortly after it occurred. Helping to treat the wounded after the shooting stopped was a young German private in the Red Cross, the Baron Erwin von Luittwitz; later he would become Defense Minister of Germany and, as a general, would lead the Kaiser's forces into Belgium. A young officer in General Miles' command, Second Lieutenant John J. Pershing, of the Sixth Cavalry, would defeat those German forces in 1918. Finally – so some believed, there was the ghost of Lieutenant Colonel George Armstrong Custer.

The violence that occurred at Wounded Knee happened where it did by accident. The nature of what occurred – a beaten civilization desperately struggling to survive, and suffering a final crushing blow by a dominant and overwhelming society – was almost predestined. It was the violent end result of westward expansion that began with the arrival of the first Europeans in the New World. This launched a new frontier age that was to be the doom of indigenous lifeways throughout North America. It ended with a final confrontation of two cultures so different that mutual understanding was improbable and coexistence impossible.

The frontier settlers of the late 1800s, for instance, saw themselves as sober, God-fearing, and industrious. They generally saw the Indians as ignorant savages – uncouth, unsanitary, and unpredictable. On the other hand, the Indians saw themselves as generous, God-fearing, honest, and self-respecting. They thought it was the white men who were uncivilized. The whites seemed like greedy, undisciplined children. They wanted to own and confine everything. Even the grass was entrapped by the whites within fences. But worst of all, from the Indians' point of view, the white men were liars. With each of their lies more of the Indians' land had been taken away, until it was nearly gone. Now the once proud tribes, including the great Lakota, could live only on barren reservations and on the white man's pitiful charity.

Then, unexpectedly, when it seemed that everything had been taken away forever, the new Messiah gave thousands of Indians, throughout much of the West, a new dream and a new hope – and the course was set for the final bloody collision at Wounded Knee.

A MESSIAH AND HIS GHOST DANCE GOSPEL

*D*espite their seeming novelty, the Ghost Dance and Messiah of 1890 were not new. The concept of a messiah or anointed deliveror was one held by many tribes and was also taught by Christians and their missionaries from the 15th century on. There had been numerous "messiahs" in the past. Frequently, when white pressure became overwhelming for a tribe or group of tribes, a special Indian prophet arose to provide comfort, a promise of relief from oppression, and a happier future. Wovoka's father was one of these prophets. It was he and his mentor, Wodziwob, who initiated, around 1870, what evolved into the Ghost Dance associated with Wounded Knee.

Born about 1857, near Walker Lake in western Nevada, Wovoka was the son of Tavibo, a renowned Paiute shaman. When Wovoka was about 12 years old, Tavibo and Wodziwob shared a special vision. A holy voice spoke to each of them, saying the old earth was tired out and God was going to renew it; but this time only for Indians. All the Indians who had died would come back to life, and all of them would be young again and would enjoy their renewed earth forever. There were two basic requirements, however. The Indians had to believe Tavibo's and Wodziwob's words firmly and had to prepare for the new world by regularly performing a sacred dance. This was the Dance of Souls Departed, or "Ghost Dance."

The prophets' vision caught on very strongly with a number of tribes in Nevada, northern California, and southern Oregon. In fact, it was likely a contributing factor in the violent "Modoc War" of 1872-1873, in the lava fields of the Oregon-California border. Shortly thereafter, and following the death from disease of Tavibo, excitement over and active participation in the early Ghost Dance disappeared among the now disillusioned believers.

When Wovoka's father died, the boy was 14 and homeless. A white ranching family, by the name of Wilson, took him in. They raised him with their own two sons, giving him the name Jack Wilson. The Wilsons were devout Christians and believed strongly in nightly bible readings attended by the whole family. This was how Wovoka gained his primary knowledge of Christianity. He was curious and went on to learn more from the Mormon missionaries proselyting among the Paiutes.

The famous "Ghost Shirts" worn by some Indians in tribes which practiced the Ghost Dance may have originated from Wovoka's experience with the Mormons. He knew that many elders with the church had special underclothes, or endowments, and that these endowments somehow promised celestial glory after death. Their sacred markings were also believed to provide certain protections against harm or evil. Wovoka reportedly made, and encouraged the making of, Indian shirt versions of holy garments. His supposed view was that these shirts were to be used as symbols of passive strength, as an aid to courage, and as a visible reminder of the great millennium that was at hand.

As a young man, Wovoka spent a couple of years working in the hop fields of Washington and Oregon. While there, he studied the new religious beliefs of several Indian groups. First, there were the Indian practitioners, mostly of the Skokomish tribe, of the white man's Shaker religion…short for "shaking Quakers." The Shakers were a Christian sect who believed, among other things, that through their dance ritual and "the agitation of the body" they received the gift of prophecy. Then there were the "Blowers," an offshoot of the Shakers. Instead of greeting a stranger with a handshake, they waved and blew at him to chase away his badness. Finally there were the "Dreamers" who followed the teachings of a regionally famous Wanapum chief and shaman named Smohalla. He and his cult had many beliefs, one being disdain for the white man's agriculture, professing the uprooting of soil as evil. The central tenet, however, was that people obtained lasting wisdom only from deep personal reflections and dreams. It could not be taught, for example, by the white man to the Indian.

Despite his keen interest in spiritual matters, when Wovoka returned to Nevada he showed no outward signs of desiring to do Indian missionary work. He married a devoted Paiute wife, settled down to being Jack Wilson, and began a period of steady employment, mainly with his adoptive family. He developed a reputation among local whites as a hard worker and solid citizen.

It seems this was a time of frustration for Wovoka. He was living much like a white man but wasn't fully accepted by white society. He was the son of a famous Paiute shaman but did not have the respect from his people he felt he deserved. Then, about 1886, things began to change. The pace was slow at first, but later it accelerated like a storm-blown prairie fire.

It started one day while Wovoka was chopping wood in the mountains. He was overwhelmed by a strange sensation, collapsed, and began to have a vision. As he told it, he died, went to heaven, was spoken to by God, and was then returned to earth and resurrected. The message of this vision was very much like the one his father had received – world renewal, brotherhood, and good times for all, and apparently including white men at first. The next day the voice of God spoke to him again and charged him with sharing the vision with his brethren. So, almost immediately, Wovoka began preaching the new order to the Paiutes. He revived his father's Ghost Dance, with some changes, but continued working for his white employers as he was not yet receiving the substantial contributions of food, clothing, and money, from other Indians, that would begin arriving after mid-summer of 1888.

After almost three years of preaching among the Paiutes and holding regular Ghost Dance ceremonies, Wovoka saw that interest in his movement had so markedly declined that he needed a miracle to keep it going. So, he performed the first of three "miracles" that progressively confirmed his legitimacy among the Paiutes and expanded his holy reputation and direct influence among thousands of Indians in a dozen western states.

Wovoka declared that on a certain day in July of 1888, in order to prove that he was indeed God's messenger, he would make ice appear in the Walker River. On the appointed day he traveled, with believers and skeptics, to the "white man's bridge" on the river. He began to pray and then appeared to go into a trance. His trance-like state continued for some time until chunks of ice actually did come floating down the river.

Whether Wovoka knew the secret of the ice or not, the onlookers didn't. The Wilson brothers, either at Wovoka's request or on their own volition – to keep their "brother" from losing face among his own people – had dumped a wagon-load of ice from their father's ice house into the Walker River some distance up-stream from the bridge. They accomplished this completely undetected. The Paiutes were duly amazed and were thoroughly convinced that Wovoka was the true prophet of God. His influence increased tremendously among the northern and southern Paiutes in Nevada and their eastern cousins in Utah, but it did not extend beyond the tribe. This, too, changed after "The Day the Sun Died."

A complete solar eclipse was experienced over the far western states on January 1, 1889. Most western Indians had no warning of the eclipse, no understanding of it, and were temporarily panicstricken. Wovoka, who was suffering in bed from a near-fatal case of what was probably scarlet fever, appeared to those around him to have died with the sun. In fact, Paiutes who had gone to his home during the eclipse to request an intercession with God were convinced he was dead and began to talk of organizing a burial. But, Wovoka's wife would not allow it. Some time after the sun came "alive" again, Wovoka also came alive. He described having ascended to heaven once more and that he had an expanded message from God.

The old world wouldn't just be renewed, it would first be *destroyed* and then replaced by a fresh, happy, and abundant one for all the Indians and their ancestors. God didn't exactly exclude the whites this time, but neither had he included them. Wovoka, himself, was given the power to control the weather, destroy the old world, and create the new one when the time was right; for he had been promoted. Wovoka was now Christ, the Son of God. Some say he later displayed the scars of the crucifixion on his hands and feet. God further ordered that Wovoka summon Indians from all the tribes to hear the new message which was, indeed, Christ-like, promoting an attitude of peace, love, and non-violence toward all, including the white man. God would deal with the whites when the time came. Wovoka's very words were: "Do no harm to no one. Do right always. Tell no lies. Never fight. Indians must no longer be afraid. The Indian dead have arisen. They wait for us with the Great Spirit. Indians must both believe and faithfully perform the sacred dance." The multi-night Ghost Dances became more frequent and impressive. Guided by Wovoka, hundreds of Indians were now dancing to exhaustion and having visions, visiting heaven, talking with their deceased loved-ones, and getting glimpses of the promised new world. Wovoka's movement was poised for national prominence. The great majority of Paiutes were unflinching disciples, ready to go on missions to other tribes. It seemed one more appropriate miracle would secure Wovoka's position and make his mission to the other Indians unstoppable.

The Walker River area was suffering from the effects of persistent drought in 1889. The Indians were especially hard hit. A captain of Indian police and skeptic, named Josephus, went to Wovoka with a well-publicized request to bring rain. Wovoka prayed on the problem for a day, and he then told the captain there would be plenty of water in three days. On the morning of the third day, Josephus and everyone else arose in awe to find the Walker River out of its banks and the lowlands flooded. The upper watershed had received a large amount of rain. Josephus now openly declared, "I am a strong believer in the unnatural powers of the new Christ." White men's declarations of coincidence went unheeded.

The mission to other tribes began in earnest. Wovoka had combined the knowledge gained from Protestants, Mormons, Shakers, Dreamers, and Blowers with his father's shamanism, and his own sleight of hand and wizardry, into a gripping and unbelievably powerful religion for a people who were desperately in need of one. His missionaries took the message to neighboring tribes and beyond.

The fuel of despair worked to carry the word of this second coming of Jesus, his plan to save the Red Man, and the paradise that would follow. Ironically, the United States government unwittingly provided a great deal of assistance in spreading the Ghost Dance religion. Wovoka, on orders from God, sent scores of letters of invitation and instruction, dictated to others, through the U.S. mail. He also mailed packages of ceremonial items for the Dance, including red ocher, holy feathers, and, occasionally, items of his personal clothing – also considered holy. In addition, many Indian messengers traveled free by rail, as was their right under treaties or other agreements with the federal government, including the Lakota – Wovoka's most famous converts.

Wovoka (seated) had chosen the spring of 1891 as the time when he would destroy the old world and create a new one for the Indian. Wovoka was photographed by James Mooney in 1891 while the latter was doing research on the Ghost Dance religion for the U.S. Bureau of Ethnology. Bailey (1970) attributes the following quotation to Mooney, as he was ending his visits with Wovoka:

"After viewing the mass graves at Grand River and Wounded Knee, and after talking to the Sioux who have lived through the killings, I am convinced that America will someday look on this past year with shame and sorrow. Now that I see you – a devout and gentle man – I am also more than ever convinced that another terrible wrong has been perpetrated against your race."

7

TATANKA YOTANKA (SITTING BULL)

*F*or the Sioux, and for other Ghost Dance followers, it was mostly the traditional people, still desperately clinging to their memories of the past, who fervently took up the practice of Wovoka's religion. By 1890, the traditionalists were often a minority within their tribes. To understand Wounded Knee, it is helpful to have a basic understanding of these people, especially those among the Sioux; and, there is no better example than Sitting Bull, who was to figure prominently in the Wounded Knee story. He was the last of the Sioux Chiefs to surrender to reservation life. In addition, even as late as 1890, his continued intransigence regarding the rightness of the old ways, and their practice, was a source of ongoing frustration for government officials and the more "progressive" Indians who had decided that acceptance of the white man's civilization was inevitable.

To review the life of Sitting Bull is akin to reviewing the life of the Teton Lakota or Plains Sioux from the glory years to the final subjugation at Wounded Knee. It is not an overstatement to suggest that, for all of his adult life, he exemplified the spiritual and fighting heart of the Lakota – who were an instinctively nomadic people, habituated to ritualized violence, and yet uniquely cultured and devoutly religious.

EARLY YEARS

Sitting Bull was probably born in 1831, on the Grand River, in what is now South Dakota. His father, Returns-Again, was a highly respected warrior of the Hunkpapa division of the Lakotah – who were among the largest of the North American Indian "nations." Sitting Bull's childhood name, as was customary with the Lakota, was different from his adult name. He was called "Slow" because of his measured and serious nature; though he was a fast learner and was physically active, earning possession of his first horse at age 10.

Childhood for Slow ended about 1845, when he was 14. He had tagged along behind his father and other warriors on a punitive raid against a band of Crow. Armed with only a coup stick, Slow galloped into the thick of the battle and rammed his stick into a Crow, knocking the warrior down just before he could fire the arrow aimed at the boy. This feat led Returns-Again to announce his son's adulthood and to name him Tatanka Yotanka, or Sitting Bull, a name which Returns-Again had been "given" by a lone buffalo bull one night near a hunting camp.

AS A WARRIOR

During the next two years, Sitting Bull achieved several milestones in his life: he killed his first buffalo bull; he completed a vision quest, through which he received an important leadership message from Wakantanka, the Great Spirit; he experienced the first of a number of painful Sun Dances; and he became a member of the Strong Heart Society. This last achievement was very significant because the Strong Hearts were the warriors who exercised control over others.

By 1856, Sitting Bull had so distinguished himself in battle that he was selected as leader of the Strong Hearts. He proved to be an outstanding war leader despite the loss, in 1857, of his father in battle, and his mother, wife, and son in a typhoid outbreak.

The first of Sitting Bull's many hostile encounters with whites, arising over the loss of land and the ruin of the Lakota's bison-based economy, happened in the early 1860s. However, the two greatest battles came years later in Montana Territory on Rosebud Creek and the Little Bighorn River.

When 1876 began, Sitting Bull was the acknowledged principal counselor and strategist of the non-treaty – or "wild" – Sioux. He and many others had refused to sign the 1868 treaty at Fort Laramie that had established "The Great Sioux Reservation." Also in 1876, the federal government, fed up with the unwillingness of the treaty Sioux to sell the Black Hills, instituted a new policy for all the Plains Sioux. The government was angry because sale of the Black Hills would allow whites to mine gold there legally. Gold had been discovered in 1874 by a military expeditionary force of 1,000 men, commanded by Lt. Col. George Custer, which had violated the 1868 treaty by entering the Black Hills without Sioux authorization. The new policy had two main points. First, all free-roaming Sioux were ordered to report to the reservation by January 31, 1876. Second, all Sioux found off the reservation after January 31 would be considered combatants and would be compelled, by military force, to return to the reservation. In the middle of the summer of 1876, all reservation Sioux were brought under the jurisdiction of the War Department, from the Interior Department, to be treated as prisoners of war until hostilities ceased, whether or not they had been hostile.

The first military attacks against off-reservation Sioux, in 1876, took place in the spring. Those who escaped, and others not yet located by the Army, sought refuge and collective protection with Sitting Bull and his strong band of Hunkpapas in the Tongue River country. Eventually, in early June of 1876, upwards of 10,000 Indians (including 3,000 warriors), representing the Hunkpapa, Blackfeet, Brulé, Sans Arc, Oglala, Minneconjou, Yanktonai, and Santee Sioux, as well as hundreds of Northern Cheyenne and some Arapaho, were traveling together in Montana.

On June 17, Sitting Bull and his fellow fugitives, including the very gifted tactician, Crazy Horse, purposely engaged and defeated General Crook's substantial force, which was searching for the Sioux, on Rosebud Creek in southeast Montana. After this great success, the jubilant Indians moved west to the Little Bighorn River, known to the Sioux as the Greasy Grass, to hunt game and graze their thousands of horses.

On June 25, 1876, Custer showed up nearby with the Seventh Cavalry. After inexplicably dividing his already small force into three units, each unit going in a different direction, he took the main body of around 250 troopers and scouts on his brash and fatal charge toward the huge Indian camp. The obliteration of Custer's command absolutely stunned and enraged the nation, which was on the eve of celebrating the centennial of the Declaration of Independence.

Following the battle, the various tribes broke camp and separated, realizing the Army would be greatly reinforced in the near future. Several bands were soon attacked and defeated by the U.S. troops; others returned voluntarily to reservation life. In the fall of 1876, reacting to Custer's defeat, the U.S. forced the Lakota on the reservation to sell the government nine million acres, including the Black Hills. Sitting Bull and his band, still at large, were chased relentlessly but were not captured. In the spring of 1877, tired of running, Sitting Bull took hundreds of his people into exile in Canada. There he hoped the white grandmother, Queen Victoria, would provide some assistance if he and his followers lived peaceably. But the Canadian government, especially with pressure from the Americans, could not acknowledge responsibility for tribal members whose reservation was in the United States.

CAPTIVITY

Starvation, illness, misery, and attrition took a heavy toll. Finally, Sitting Bull and his small band could resist no longer. On July 19, 1881, the chief and 186 of his remaining followers crossed into the U.S. and surrendered at Fort Buford, Dakota Territory, where Sitting Bull stated: "Let it be recorded that I am the last of my people to lay down my gun." He was not pardoned, as promised, but was arrested and transported to Fort Randall, Dakota Territory, where he stayed for two years as a military prisoner. (Apparently developed at this time was his well-known song of lament, now in the Bureau of Ethnology Collection, which employed a series of sad vocalizations and whose core words were: "I-ki-ci-ze wa-on kon   he wa-na he-na-la ye-lo   he i-yo-ti-ye ki-ya wa-on" – A warrior I have been. Now, it is all over. A hard time I have.)

In 1883, Sitting Bull was transferred to Standing Rock Reservation, Dakota Territory, and the jurisdiction of the Department of the Interior. He had become somewhat of a celebrity during his captivity and, in 1884, made a government-authorized tour of 15 American cities. Then Buffalo Bill Cody gained permission from the Interior Department for Sitting Bull to tour the U.S. and Canada with his Wild West Show in 1885.

An 1887 invitation to the elder chief to tour Europe was turned down. New attempts to take more land from the Sioux kept Sitting Bull at home so that he could try to wield his remaining influence over his people. His goal was to discourage them from agreeing to any government offers to buy more land. The government's agents outmaneuvered Sitting Bull, however, and the land cession of 1889 was made, dividing the large reservation into six smaller ones.

In the fall of 1890, the Ghost Dance came to Standing Rock Reservation. Major responsibility for the misunderstood movement was wrongly attributed to Sitting Bull by many whites. He was, nonetheless, very much interested in the new religion and directly or indirectly encouraged its practice by his several hundred remaining followers. Sitting Bull's death, resulting from the Ghost Dance movement, is discussed, in context, in the following section.

The killing of Sitting Bull was one of the events which led directly to the incident at Wounded Knee. His so-called "hostile and non-progressive" attitude, maintained after his surrender, is stated below.

God made me an Indian, but not a reservation Indian.

I wish all to know that I do not propose to sell any part of my country.

What treaty that the white man ever made with us has he kept? Not one. When I was a boy the Sioux owned the world; the sun rose and set on their land; they sent ten thousand men to battle. Where are the warriors today? Who slew them? Where are our lands? Who owns them? What white man can ever say I stole his land...? Yet they say I am a bad Indian...Is it wrong for me to love my own? Is it wicked for me because my skin is red? Because I am a Sioux; because I was born where my father lived; because I would die for my people and my country?

– CHIEF SITTING BULL

11

LAKOTA GHOST DANCERS
AND WHITE REACTIONS

Wovoka's wondrous news reached the Pine Ridge and Rosebud Reservations (see map on page 18) during the summer of 1889, in bits and pieces, by messengers and letters from other tribes. There was much doubt, mixed with a great deal of hopeful curiosity. So, in the fall, the chiefs who were interested met at Pine Ridge Reservation and appointed a delegation to go west and see the new Indian Messiah, or "Wanekia."

The delegation went mainly by train, stopping periodically to visit other tribes. They were joined by more Indians along the way. When Wovoka's Nevada home was finally reached, the delegation found that their group was part of a much larger gathering of representatives from many tribes. Everyone was very eager to begin learning from the Indian savior.

Members of the Lakota delegation were gone from their reservations all winter and did not get back to Pine Ridge until April of 1890. After their return, the chiefs called a council. The Indian agent, however, got wind of something happening, though he did not understand what, and had several delegation members arrested and confined for a few days. He released them on the promise that no councils would be held to discuss their trip.

Meanwhile, delegates Kicking Bear and Short Bull spread the message, and a big council was called far away from agency headquarters. The Messiah's words were shared from a letter, along with wonderful stories about the trip and personal Ghost Dance experiences. The delegation members were interweaving dreams and reality in their report, with little attempt to separate the two. As the council developed, Kicking Bear, the most militant member of the delegation, became the main spokesman for the group. He clearly reveled in the message and his role in bringing it to the People. Thereafter, Kicking Bear, joined by Short Bull in somewhat of a support role, was the primary apostle of the Ghost Dance among the Lakota.

Kicking Bear's primacy was unfortunate because the very peaceful message of love, kindness, and patience from Wovoka was misinterpreted into a more militant and potentially hostile theme. Kicking Bear related that "when the dancers [in Nevada] came back from visiting the ghosts…they brought back [stories of] water, and fire, and wind with which to kill all the whites or Indians who help the chief of the whites." He also described the "holy shirts," used by some Ghost Dancers, and said that bullets would not go through them and they were made "for war." No other tribes had "bulletproof" shirts as part of their Ghost Dance, though they had holy garments.

The Ghost Dance spread around Pine Ridge and the Rosebud Reservation, but the nice weather and better times of late spring, compared with the tough winter, were not conducive to missionary work. Nonetheless, dances were organized in various locations and participation was relatively good. Some off-reservation whites were beginning to show concern with the recent zealous activity they observed among their "wild neighbors." But those in charge, like Agent Gallagher of Pine Ridge, felt the new religion would die out, "as soon as the Indians find there is no truth to all these fantastic stories." Even so, one concerned citizen of Pierre, South Dakota, wrote the Secretary of the Interior on May 29, 1890, to say that he had good information the Sioux were secretly planning an outbreak in the coming months. The Secretary reacted to this by immediately requesting reports from the agents in charge on the Sioux reservations. Each agent replied that everything was "business as usual," causing the issue to be tabled at Interior.

As summer developed, a serious drought settled in. Then, the already low rations were cut again by the government. At about the same time, Washington ordered that the Sioux could no longer hunt game. This order was not at all well received by those Sioux who supplemented their meager rations with game.

Though missionary work went a bit slowly for Kicking Bear and Short Bull in the spring, by late July and early August hungry, disappointed, and angry Lakota were joining the Ghost Dancers in droves. Participation was increased by the fact that, unlike most other Lakota dances, everyone was welcome to join in. The large circles of dancers included men, women, little children, and even feeble older people with canes.

After the Pine Ridge and Rosebud Reservations became active centers for the Ghost Dance, Kicking Bear decided to take the theology to his own Minneconjou people on the Cheyenne River Reservation. He did not have much success, with two very notable exceptions – the people of Chief Hump and Chief Big Foot, the most traditional bands on the reservation, adopted the Ghost Dance quickly and enthusiastically. Within Big Foot's band was the medicine man Yellow Bird, a key figure at Wounded Knee. Yellow Bird was considered one of the most anti-white and traditional of all the Lakota. He was also known to be a skilled agitator and kept Big Foot's people so engrossed with the new religion that one observer noted they danced "both day and night, so long as they are able to move and to keep awake."

September passed with Indians dancing on the southern Sioux reservations by the hundreds. Still the Ghost Dance had not reached north to the Hunkpapa on Standing Rock Reservation. But, in early October, Kicking Bear received six Hunkpapa messengers who carried a request from Sitting Bull to bring word of the Ghost Dance. On October 9, Kicking Bear paid a visit to Sitting Bull at the Grand River camp. He told of his trip to Wovoka's country, of visits with the Messiah, of talks with the dead, and of Wovoka's promise of a new and abundant world where the Red Man could live as he did before the white settlers came. Sitting Bull listened, only half believing, but also desiring to raise the morale of his followers who did not want to miss out on the Messiah's promise. Therefore, he invited Kicking Bear to stay and teach the Ghost Dance. Sitting Bull apparently even participated until ordered by the Indian agent to cease.

By mid-October the Ghost Dance had spread to 12 states and more than 30 tribes, with many more potential converts. Confused and irritated Indian agents and Army officers, from the Dakotas to Arizona and from Indian Territory to Nevada, were trying to discern the meaning of it all. Formerly hostile tribes were dancing a great deal, and many of their past dances had been "war" dances. Also, why did the Sioux make "bulletproof" shirts unless they expected to engage in battle? By early autumn the official order came from Washington to stop the Ghost Dance.

A week after arriving at Standing Rock, Kicking Bear was escorted off the reservation by armed Indian police, under orders from Agent McLaughlin. On October 17, McLaughlin notified the Commissioner of Indian Affairs that "Sitting Bull is high priest and leading apostle of this latest Indian absurdity...Sitting Bull is a polygamist, libertine, habitual liar, active obstructionist, and great obstacle to the civilization of these people...I would respectfully request the removal from the reservation and confinement in some military prison...of Sitting Bull and the

Arapaho Ghost Dancers – Men and women were both involved in Ghost Dancing. Here some Arapahos are singing and dancing with arms raised while other Ghost Dancers sit watching. The dancers' goal was to dance until exhausted and entranced, for in their trances their spirits visited Wovoka's promised paradise. The bird symbol painted on the back of the man in the left foreground may represent the crow or eagle, sacred to the Ghost Dancers.

parties named in my letter of June 18," which included Big Foot of the Cheyenne River Reservation. Nothing happened right away.

By mid-November the Ghost Dance was so prevalent on some of the Sioux reservations that many other activities came to a halt. Children stopped going to school, normally busy trading posts were empty of customers, and little or no work was being done on the small Indian farms. Various bands of hundreds of Indians were migrating to the more distant corners of several reservations to practice the Ghost Dance without interference from Indian agents and police.

The whole region was now astir. National newspapers were getting heavily involved and, in competition with each other, manufactured stories where none could be found. They were a major and unnecessary cause of regional panic and pressure on the government for military intervention. Some of the spurious headlines read:

MESSIAH EXPECTED TO ARRIVE AT PINE RIDGE TODAY,
WHEN THE SAVAGES WILL FIGHT

LOSS OF LIFE REPORTED

OLD SITTING BULL STIRRING UP THE EXCITED REDSKINS

REDSKINS BLOODY WORK

The new, easily intimidated, inexperienced, and very frightened Indian Agent Royer, at Pine Ridge, believing all rumors, telegraphed Washington with the message: "The Indians are dancing in the snow and are wild and crazy...We need protection and we need it now...I deem the situation at this agency very critical, and believe that an outbreak may occur at any time, and it does not seem to me safe to longer withhold troops...." He got results.

On November 14, the agents on the four affected reservations – Pine Ridge, Rosebud, Cheyenne River, and Standing Rock – received from the Interior Secretary this message: "The President has directed the Secretary of War to assume a military responsibility for the suppression of any threatened out-break among the Indians." Then, on the 20th, the Indian Bureau ordered the same agents to telegraph the names of "fomenters of disturbances" among the Ghost Dancers. A list was compiled in Washington and sent to General Nelson Miles, commander of the military district of the Missouri, at his headquarters in Chicago.

General Miles found Sitting Bull's name on the list of "fomenters" and assumed he was to blame for all the unrest. The general knew that a forced arrest by soldiers would create trouble. A quiet arrest was preferred. To accomplish this he contacted Buffalo Bill Cody, one of the few white men who Sitting Bull ever liked. Cody assured the general that, by combining persuasion with presents, he was certain he could bring in the chief peacefully. An appropriate order for Cody was subsequently issued by General Miles.

When Buffalo Bill arrived at Standing Rock with his entourage, he was met by a doubting Agent McLaughlin. Apprehensive that Cody would fail at the arrest attempt and only make things worse, the agent implored Washington to have Cody withdrawn from the scene. At the very last moment he succeeded. President Harrison personally rescinded General Miles' order by telegram on November 29. Thus Cody, without ever seeing Sitting Bull, was required to leave Standing Rock and return to Chicago.

At Pine Ridge Agency, the Army had arrived from Nebraska during the night of November 19-20 and set up camp by dawn. The surprised Indians learned that hasty rail transport and a forced night march brought the soldiers among them so quickly. This new twist to the situation created a great deal of tension and dismay for the Indians because they now knew for certain the Department of the Interior was no longer in control at Pine Ridge. Dr. Valentine McGillycuddy, a former Indian agent, had been sent to Pine Ridge by the governor of South Dakota, when the Army was deployed, to assess the trouble and advise the Army on the governor's behalf. He concluded, "I should let the dance continue. The coming of the troops has frightened the Indians. If the Seventh-day Adventists prepare their ascension robes for the second coming of the Savior, the United States Army is not put in motion to prevent them. Why should the Indians not have the same privilege? If the troops remain, trouble is sure to come." The doctor's viewpoint was ignored and the tension grew.

The moment the Army detachment had arrived at Pine Ridge the commanding officer sent messengers to all outlying camps on the reservation with word that he wanted the people to come in immediately to the agency and camp there. Everyone who did would receive protection and increased rations. Those who did not come in would receive no rations. In response, most of the people in the outlying camps, already suffering from hunger, came to the agency, thus giving up the Ghost Dance dream forever. Many did not come in, however.

In the first week of December most of the remaining bands of Ghost Dancers joined together in the Bad Lands, in the northwest corner of Pine Ridge Reservation. Up to several thousand Lakota, under Kicking Bear, Short Bull, Two Strike, and other chiefs, were camped on a remote plateau stronghold, participating in the Ghost Dance and waiting for the coming of Christ and his new world. They included mostly people from the Pine Ridge and Rosebud Reservations. All were determined not to be interfered with.

On December 11, Sitting Bull requested permission from Agent McLaughlin to go to Pine Ridge Reservation, presumably to visit the Ghost Dancers. This was the last straw for government officials regarding Sitting Bull. On the 12th, the commander at Fort Yates received orders from General Miles "to secure the person of Sitting Bull. Call on the Indian agent to cooperate and render such assistance as will best promote the purpose in view." Brown (1970) describes events as follows:

> *Just before daybreak on December 15, 1890, forty-three Indian police surrounded Sitting Bull's log cabin. Three miles away a squadron of cavalry waited as a support force if needed. Lieutenant Bull Head, the*

Indian policeman in charge of the party, found Sitting Bull asleep on the floor. When he was awakened, the chief stared incredulously at Bull Head. "What do you want here?" he asked.

"You are my prisoner," said Bull Head. "You must go to the agency."

Sitting Bull yawned and sat up. "All right," he replied, "let me put on my clothes and I'll go with you." He asked the policeman to have his horse saddled.

When Bull Head emerged from the cabin with Sitting Bull he found a crowd of Ghost Dancers gathering outside. They outnumbered the police four to one. Catch-the-Bear, one of the dancers [who had an old grievance against Bull Head] moved toward Bull Head. "You think you are going to take him," Catch-the-Bear shouted. "You shall not do it!"

"Come now," Bull Head said quietly to his prisoner, "do not listen to anyone." But Sitting Bull [loudly implored by his followers not to go] held back, making it necessary for Bull Head and Sergeant Red Tomahawk to force him toward his horse.

At this moment, Catch-the-Bear threw off his blanket and brought up a rifle. He fired at Bull Head, wounding him in the side. As Bull Head fell, he tried to shoot his assailant, but the bullet struck Sitting Bull instead. Almost simultaneously, Red Tomahawk shot Sitting Bull through the head and killed him.

When Sitting Bull fell, a wild fight erupted. The Ghost Dancers attacked the police with guns, knives, and clubs so forcefully that the police had to retreat back into Sitting Bull's cabin; but not before one of them escaped to fetch reinforcements. The waiting cavalry detachment arrived and, from a distance, fired several explosive Hotchkiss rounds into the open ground between the police position and the Indians. At that, most of Sitting Bull's people fled – though a number returned peacefully a short time later. Some 200 kept on going, headed toward the Minneconjou camps 90 miles to the south…far from the scene at Sitting Bull's camp where 14 people now lay dead or dying, including six policemen.

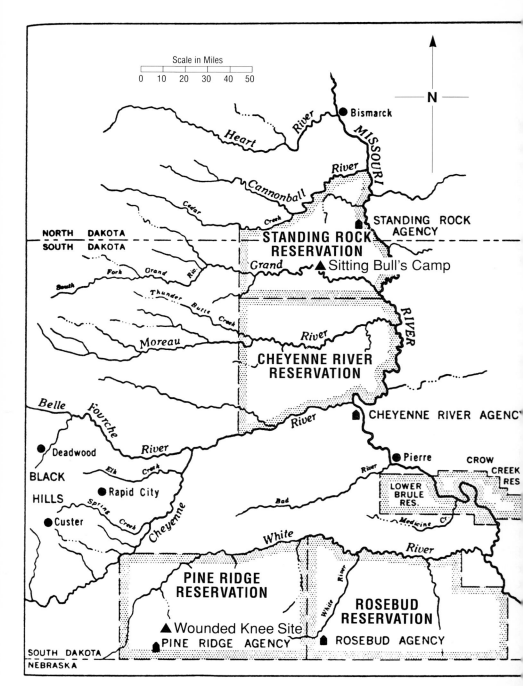

This map of the Sioux Reservation, showing Sitting Bull's camp and the Wounded Knee battlefield site, is adapted from Mooney (1896) and Utley (1963).

FLIGHT AND DEATH

Between December 15 and 29, 1890, a complicated and controversial series of events involving the Army, the Interior Department, Indians, politicians, settlers, celebrities, publicity seekers, newspapers, and others culminated in the Wounded Knee tragedy.

On December 17, the cold and starving refugees from Sitting Bull's camp began to arrive in Chief Hump's Minneconjou settlement on the Cheyenne River. At about the same time, General Miles sent Captain Ewers, Hump's old friend from Army scouting days in the late 1870s, to talk to the feared chief and encourage him to surrender to Army custody at Fort Bennett. Hump, to the surprise of everyone, readily agreed. He said he would take all his people in and would even sign up as a scout to help bring in other Ghost Dancers.

Most of Sitting Bull's Hunkpapas decided to go with Hump. But, the night before the trek (the night of December 18), about 40 Hunkpapas and 30 of Hump's young warriors decided to sneak out and go west to find Big Foot's "free" Minneconjou band.

Three days earlier, Big Foot, not knowing he was on the "fomenters" list, had decided to head east to Fort Bennett to pick up badly needed rations and annuities. Before doing so, he visited Colonel Sumner at the Eighth Cavalry's new battalion bivouac several miles up-stream from his own camp. There he personally told the Colonel of his plans in order to prevent misinterpretation of his movements. Colonel Sumner deferred to Big Foot's apparent sincerity and determined to let the Indians travel to the fort unescorted.

On the 17th, after Big Foot's band had left, Colonel Sumner received word to arrest and hold the Indians until further orders. As for Big Foot's group, they were now breaking camp 30 or so miles east and had just encountered the Hunkpapa refugees and Hump's warriors.

Big Foot and his people listened to the stories of Sitting Bull's death and the ensuing fight. Fear, confusion, and anger raged through the camp. The Lakota performed the Ghost Dance and mourned Sitting Bull the rest of that day. The following morning, Big Foot and his counselors decided that Fort Bennett was the place to go – the Army and Hump's defection were too much to have to face at this very difficult time. They gathered their belongings and continued east. But, two days later, on the 21st, Colonel Sumner and the Eighth Cavalry caught up with and arrested them. The detachment had orders to take the band back up-river, probably to Fort Meade in the Black Hills.

When the westward-traveling column passed closely by Big Foot's settlement, the Indians rushed into their respective cabins for warmth and rest. Colonel Sumner, now quite concerned about the probable difficulty of being able to dislodge the people from their homes, shared with Big Foot the new orders he had just received. The Eighth was to turn the entire procession around and travel to Fort Bennett. The Colonel allowed the Indians one night in their cabins, strongly emphasizing the mandatory departure the following morning. Taking Big Foot's word that all would cooperate, Colonel Sumner withdrew his command several miles up-stream to his original bivouac area.

That night, riders informed Big Foot of a second Army column coming up-river toward them. Though he told those around him he did not want to break his word to Colonel Sumner, Big Foot, fearful the Army was moving in for a big kill of Ghost Dancers, chose to flee. Without any sleep, the captives hastily loaded everything they could into wagons and on travois and struck out south on a trail through a portion of the Bad Lands. Their eventual goal was to reach protection under the famous Chief Red Cloud, at Pine Ridge, who had a good reputation for dealing with the whites. (On the way, a group of about 60 broke off – after much arguing – with the intention of finding and joining Kicking Bear. They never did and were captured, without incident, the day after the killings at Wounded Knee.) Now looking for Big Foot, as a result of Colonel Sumner's report to General Miles of the chief's escape, were the Eighth Cavalry battalion, the Fort Bennett column, a Sixth Cavalry troop, and Seventh Cavalry battalions. The latter had been quickly dispatched from Pine Ridge, having initially arrived from Fort Riley, Kansas, at the end of November. The Seventh including five officers who were veterans of Custer's divided command at the Little Bighorn, was to execute a flanking maneuver in the hope of locating Big Foot and preventing him from hooking up with Kicking Bear and the other Ghost Dancers on their plateau stronghold.

As Big Foot was heading south, Kicking Bear and scores of vengeful warriors, now reacting to news of Sitting Bull's death, had taken to sniping at and directly attacking white ranchers and small Army detachments in the region just outside the Bad Lands. This heightened worries about a large-scale outbreak and intensified the effort to capture Big Foot. By Christmas day, Big Foot had developed pneumonia and decided to camp briefly at a place called Cedar Spring. He ordered the young horses killed to feed his starving people and sent several riders to Pine Ridge. They were to inform the chiefs of his plans to travel there in peace and that he was very ill.

Following a fierce storm that night, the messengers returned just as camp was breaking. They brought word that Kicking Bear and Short Bull, after the appeals of several Indian peace delegations, had agreed to come in from the Bad Lands and surrender on the 29th. The Pine Ridge chiefs recommended that Big Foot arrive at the same time. They also suggested that, to avoid the Seventh Cavalry troops now camped at Wounded Knee, he should swing wide to the southeast and then turn west to Pine Ridge. Big Foot, now coughing up blood, was too ill for the extra travel. He decided to take the direct route to Pine Ridge and chance meeting up with the soldiers.

On the morning of the 28th, Big Foot's people broke camp and started what they hoped would be the last leg of their journey to safety. In the late morning they were about ten miles east of Wounded Knee when Big Foot's scouts surprised and captured four scouts from Major Whitside's Seventh Cavalry battalion. Two of the Cavalry scouts were detained and the other two were sent back to the troops. The latter two scouts had a message from the chief – that he was coming to the soldier's camp in peace. Major Whitside mounted up his battalon and led the men out to intercept Big Foot. When contact was made, the soldiers went into battle formation. At this, many of the refugees began waving flour sacks, and anything else white, as flags of truce. Big Foot then went forward to parley.

The Major demanded Big Foot's unconditional surrender, which he got. The troopers then formed a column-of-fours ahead of and behind the hungry and exhausted Indians. Big Foot was given an Army ambulance in which to travel. Then the entire cavalcade started for the battalion bivouac at Wounded Knee.

Arriving late in the day, the Indians began setting up tipis, collecting their horses, and surveying the surroundings, which were unfamiliar to most of them. It soon became obvious that the Seventh Cavalry was not going to allow any freedom like the Eighth Cavalry had and that security was going to be extremely tight. Troopers were soon on all sides. Also, the gun mules were led up a low hill to the northwest of the flat where the Indians were camped. Two rapid-fire Hotchkiss cannons were unloaded from the animals and deployed where they could cover the Indian campground. The people were scared, but Yellow Bird, the medicine man, repeatedly declared to one family after another, "Do not be afraid. Their bullets cannot harm us."

Colonel Forsyth arrived that night with the remainder of the Seventh Cavalry from Pine Ridge and took over command at Wounded Knee. He deployed his troops with Whitside's around the Indian camp and added his two Hotchkiss guns to the light artillery battery. His orders from headquarters were: "Disarm the Indians. Take every precaution to prevent their escape. If they choose to fight, destroy them." Forsyth recognized the need to wait until morning for disarming the captives. He had Big Foot moved into a troop tent with a stove and then directed the Army physician to tend to the critically ill chief. Army rations were also distributed to all the captives, but the Indians' movements were severely restricted. Though tensions were high, by late evening the Indian and cavalry camps settled in to a relatively calm night.

A bugle announced daybreak, which was comparatively mild, promising an unseasonably pleasant day. Rations were distributed to the Indians for breakfast. While they were eating, Colonel Forsyth and his officers pondered the coming disarmament. They were uncertain how many firearms the captives had but were convinced a number of the men possessed Winchester repeating rifles.

After breakfast, all of the Indian men and older boys were seated in a semicircle near Big Foot's tent. The chief remained inside for awhile but was later brought out, accompanied by the physician. Big Foot was propped up on the ground, for he could no longer stand or sit unaided. Colonel Forsyth, several officers, two reporters, an interpreter, and a Catholic priest were near Big Foot's tent. Forsyth had made a little speech, which was repeated in Lakota by the interpreter. He told the Indians they would receive increased rations, they were now safe, and the soldiers were their friends. But, to prevent any unintentional fighting from breaking out, it would be necessary for the Lakota to hand over their guns.

This disarmament request was met by much grumbling. For an Indian man to give up his gun meekly was an insult. Also, the Lakota feared they would be giving up their final means of protecting themselves. Even so, a couple of old rifles were surrendered. The officers were not at all satisfied, but the Indians continued to deny they had any more arms. A search of the Indian camp was ordered. Officers went through the tipis while enlisted men ravaged through the outside areas. The search resulted in the collection of a pile of axes, hatchets, butcher knives, tent pegs, and a little less than 40 rifles – many of the latter in bad shape. The Indians in the council area and the camp were becoming very anxious.

Agitation was growing among the captive men and they started milling around. Yellow Bird was moving around the semi-circle. He raised his arms in the direction of the Messiah, began a Ghost Dance, and threw dust into the air …the symbol of the coming destruction of the old world and the white man. He also chanted warnings and encouragement to the warriors:

Don't be afraid! Let your hearts be strong to meet what is before you!
There are lots of soldiers and they have lots of bullets, but the prairie is
large and the bullets will not go toward you, but over the large prairies.

When the interpreter related what Yellow Bird was up to, the Colonel ordered that the medicine man be seated. Just then an Indian was discovered to have a rifle under his blanket. It was confiscated and all the men were ordered to file past two inspection lines and to open their blankets. Twenty of the older men did so and proved to be unarmed. Several young men were coerced through the line and two had rifles. This was when everything rapidly fell apart.

Yellow Bird had started his Ghost Dance again, along with more strong exhortations to the young warriors. One warrior named Black Coyote – said to be deaf, on seeing the guns being taken away, took his new Winchester from under his blanket and raised it over his head. He yelled, in Lakota, that he had paid much money for the rifle and he would not give it up unless he was paid back. He moved off to the side where two sergeants slipped up behind and seized him. An angry scuffle ensued, during which the gun went off. Troopers instantly shouldered their weapons. Just as quickly, the small number of warriors who had firearms revealed them from under their blankets. There was an immediate crash of gunfire, joined by both sides. Most of the Lakota men in the semi-circle were killed outright. Many, such as Big Foot, were killed while they were sitting on the ground. Because of the poor deployment of troops, some of the bullets that missed Indians went on to strike soldiers. The entire situation had become a violent, loud, and bloody mess. Brown (1970) describes it further:

Then there was a brief lull in the rattle of arms, with small groups of
Indians and soldiers grappling at close quarters, using knives, clubs, and
pistols. As few of the Indians had arms, they soon had to flee (toward the
tipis where the women and children were), and then the big Hotchkiss
guns on the hill opened up on them, [the combined guns] firing almost a
shell a second, raking the Indian camp, shredding the tepees with flying
shrapnel, killing men, women, and children.

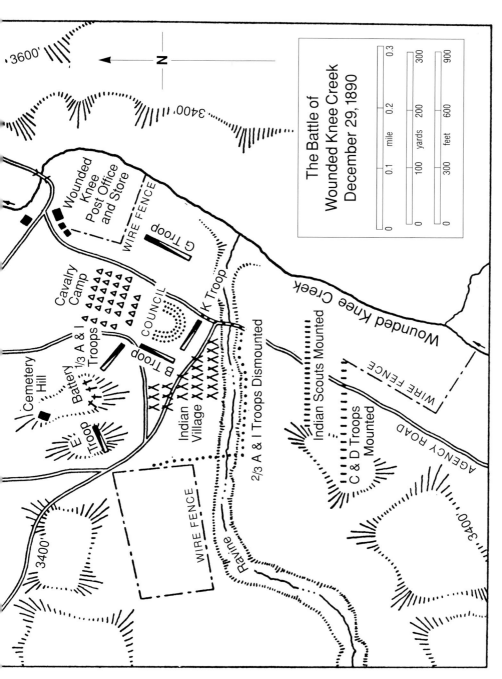

This map of the Wounded Knee battlefield site is adapted from Mooney (1896) and Utley (1963).

Among the Indian men who escaped from the council area to the camp were several who had rifles, including Yellow Bird. They kept up a brief running fight. Yellow Bird ducked into a tipi and continued to shoot at the soldiers until a Hotchkiss shell exploded and ignited the canvas. He was then struck and killed by numerous bullets – which he had heretofore believed could not harm him.

While they were firing, many of the soldiers, most of whom were green recruits, were said to have yelled repeatedly, "Remember the Little Big horn" or "Remember Custer."

Active or threatening resistance by the Indians had mostly faded after the first intense minutes. But the soldiers kept up their shooting and cannon fire. The Indian men who were still alive and mobile tried to reach the dry ravine to the south of the camp. Some of them made it, only to find it was occupied by many terrified women and children who had preceded them. Then, the ravine occupants, still in a terrible crossfire that was rapidly reducing their numbers, ran in a westerly direction attempting to reach a small stand of pines near the head of the ravine several hundred yards away. The Hotchkiss guns, finished with the camp, began firing in the ravine – which was now a death trap. A few people ran off in different directions, only to be ridden down. Troops were covering any escape route they could find, flushing scattered survivors from cover and into the line of fire. Amidst the killing, however, a number of women and children were saved by courageous Sioux scouts, some of whom were mistakenly killed or wounded by soldiers.

When the firing died away, cries of wounded Indians and soldiers came from all quarters. Officers were giving commands at the same time death songs were being chanted. The main interpreter called out that all who were still alive were to get up or waive their arms. On the edge of the ravine, a Lakota man raised himself up on his hands just as a mounted platoon came riding in from a distance. They had not yet received a cease fire order and thus opened up on the wounded Indian, killing him. Colonel Forsyth then screamed, "For God's sake! Stop shooting them!"

It was over.

POSTSCRIPT

CASUALTIES

When the shooting stopped, Army personnel gathered up their 39 wounded and 25 dead. Six of the wounded were to die later. Among the Lakota there were 51 wounded - four men and 47 women and children, some of whom also died later. The Indian dead were left on the field because a blizzard was developing. On January 1 and 2, a burial party returned to Wounded Knee and collected about 150 Indian corpses and placed them in a mass grave on the hill where the Hotchkiss guns had been positioned. Some mortally wounded Indians had crawled off to die elsewhere, while other dead had been taken away the night of the 29th by Indians from Pine Ridge. Many historians estimate the total Lakota dead to have been approximately 300. A few wounded who were missed on the 29th survived the blizzard. Included were a three-month-old girl found under the snow in a blanket beside her slain mother, and a badly wounded woman and her two wounded boys. This suggests that other potential survivors among the wounded froze to death.

Burial party on January 1 or 2, 1891, piling frozen bodies on wagons to be transported to a mass grave on the hill where the rapid-fire Hotchkiss cannons had been deployed. Burial party member Dr. Charles A. Eastman, a medical doctor (of Santee Sioux heritage) and Agency Physician, later recounted:

"Fully three miles from the scene of the massacre we found the body of a woman completely covered with a blanket of snow, and from this point [traveling toward Wounded Knee] we found them scattered along as they had been relentlessly hunted down and slaughtered while fleeing for their lives. Some of our people discovered relatives or friends among the dead, and there was much wailing and mourning. When we reached the spot where the Indian camp had stood, among the fragments of burned tents and other belongings we saw the frozen bodies lying close together or piled one upon another."

Official U.S. records do not refer to Wounded Knee as a massacre.

CONTINUED FIGHTING

News of Wounded Knee traveled immediately to Pine Ridge. Nearly 4,000 Siou
packed up their lodges and moved to more remote locations to stay out of harm's way
However, some 150 Oglala and Brulé warriors rode from Pine Ridge to Wounded Kne
to retaliate. They had a brief battle with a small group of soldiers and rescued about 2
Minneconjou survivors before riding off. The Ghost Dancers with Kicking Bear an
Short Bull, nearly at Pine Ridge on their way to surrender, got word of the killings a
Wounded Knee. They turned and went to White Clay Creek, about 15 miles from th
agency, to establish a camp and consolidate their forces with others bent on resistin
the Army. Meanwhile, Two Strike led an attack on Pine Ridge Agency and attempted t
set it on fire before fleeing with almost his entire band to the camp at White Clay Creek
Several skirmishes between warriors from the camp, settlers, and soldiers occurrec
over the next 10 to 12 days. In one, the Seventh Cavalry was surrounded while o
patrol and had to be rescued by the Ninth Cavalry. Casualties during the 12-day perio
included one civilian and three soldiers killed and five soldiers wounded. The Indian
had similar losses.

FINAL SURRENDER

Dissension among the resisting bands, hunger, low supplies, winter weather, and th
Army's ever-tightening noose around the White Clay camp forced a very hard decisior
they could no longer hold out against the whites. On January 15, 1891, Kicking Bear an
4,000 others, including 1,000 warriors, surrendered to General Miles and his troops a
Pine Ridge Agency. This brought to an end the very last of the U.S. military campaign
against tribes of Native Americans.

WILD WEST SHOW

General Miles arrested and imprisoned the 25 most prominent Ghost Dancers, intend
ing they should be held for two years. After only two months, however, Buffalo Bil
Cody secured the prisoners' release through the Secretary of War and hired the Indian
for a foreign tour of his Wild West Show. Thus, Kicking Bear, Short Bull, Two Strike
and the others (who had feared they would be hanged) made some good money and
saw Europe for a year before being returned to their reservations as "free" men. In 1899
Kicking Bear kept Indian police from taking his children away to school by holding
rifle on the officers. After police reported the incident, local federal authorities decidec
to ignore the law, in this one case, and left the chief and his children alone. Kicking Bea
died in 1904 at the age of 58.

COLONEL FORSYTH

General Miles removed Colonel Forsyth from command of the Seventh Cavalry afte
Wounded Knee and accused him of allowing the massacre of non-combatant womer
and children and of deploying his troops in a way that caused them to fire on one
another. The Colonel was exonerated by a military court of inquiry.

MEDALS

Eighteen Congressional Medals of Honor, about the only medal for valor the U.S. hac
at the time, were awarded to troopers for their actions at Wounded Knee.

MESSIAH

When Wovoka heard of the killings at Wounded Knee he pulled his blanket over hi
head and mourned in silence for some time. As the first months of 1891 passed, th

Messiah received a flood of letters from followers begging him to hasten his promised paradise. Springtime came and went with no new millennium. Wovoka had to retreat from his promise and announce, "My children, today I call upon you to travel a new trail, the only trail now open – the white man's road." He fast faded into obscurity among whites. In the 1920s, however, he was a consultant for a little-known Hollywood movie that touched on the Ghost Dance movement. Many had called Wovoka a fraud, but among his followers...greatly reduced in number after Wounded Knee and the failed promise of paradise...he remained a respected holy man. Up until his death in Yerington, Nevada, on October 4, 1932, Wovoka continued to receive occasional visits, letters, and gifts from hopeful Indians.

GHOST DANCE

Wovoka's movement abruptly ended among the Sioux in the days following Wounded Knee. At its height the dance was practiced by Native Americans in parts of each of these states: Arizona, California, Colorado, Idaho, Kansas, Montana, Nebraska, Nevada, New Mexico, North Dakota, Oklahoma, South Dakota, Texas, Utah, and Wyoming. Tribes known to have been involved in practicing the Ghost Dance then included: Assiniboine, Bannock, Caddo, Chemehuevi, Comanche, Delaware, Gosiute, Gros Ventre, Havasupai, Iowa, Kansa, Kiowa, Kiowa Apache, Kitsai, Mission, Missouri, Mohave, Northern Arapaho, Northern Cheyenne, Oto, Paiute, Pawnee, Pit River, Ponca, Shoshoni, Sioux, Southern Arapaho, Southern Cheyenne, Ute, Walapai, and Wichita.

Ghost Dancers in Indian Territory, now Oklahoma, remained the strongest adherents, but their enthusiasm fell off after February 1891 when a messenger returned from a very disappointing visit to Wovoka. Nonetheless, a major revival of the dance occurred briefly among the Kiowa in September 1894. Other tribes, like the Pawnee, were continuing the dance well into the first decade of the 1900s. Fragments of the Ghost Dance survive even today as parts of other ceremonials among some of the Plains tribes.

In 1973, Indians and others associated with the American Indian Movement occupied the community of Wounded Knee to protest the plight of Lakota on the Pine Ridge Reservation and Native Americans everywhere. Part of their activities during the occupation included participation in the Ghost Dance. Rumors circulating in the West in early 1990 indicated that Ghost Dances might be held on several reservations in recognition of the Wounded Knee Centennial. Whether or not this occurred was unknown to the author at the time of publication.

BUFFALO BILL CODY

In 1913, Buffalo Bill dreamed up the idea of making a movie of the Wounded Knee battle. He persuaded many Army and Indian veterans of the Sioux Ghost Dance campaign to appear in it. Short Bull and a few other old warriors got worked up and discussed exchanging live bullets for the blank ammunition they were to be issued, with the thought of getting revenge for Wounded Knee against the Seventh Cavalry. Cody heard of the plan and talked the Indians out of entertaining any such actions. The film was made without trouble, but its fate seems to have been lost to history. Cody died in Denver on January 10, 1917.

SITTING BULL

The dead chief's body was battered by angry Indian police and a distraught relative of one of the dead Indian policemen. It was then hauled to Fort Yates in North Dakota and buried in quicklime, without ceremony or mourners. Years later, Sitting Bull's relatives tried to have his remains moved to an area closer to his old camp on the Grand River in South Dakota. North Dakota's governors repeatedly refused over the years. One night in 1953, Sitting Bull's 79-year-old nephew (a witness to the chief's killing) led a group of South Dakotans to the Fort Yates grave. They dug up the remains and took them to Mobridge, South Dakota, where they were reburied in a steel crypt encased in concrete.

REMEMBRANCE 1990

On September 25, 1990, the Lakota people proposed legislation to the U.S. Congress. They asked for three things: compensation for damages sustained by their people at Wounded Knee in 1890, a national monument to be built for their slain ancestors, and an apology from the United States Government. In October, Congress passed a resolution expressing the government's "deep regret" for the bloodshed that ended the Indian wars on December 29, 1890. The word "apology" had been stricken from the draft the descendants wanted passed. At this printing, no action has been taken on the other requests.

Beginning December 23, 1990, several hundred people, including some descendants of the victims of Wounded Knee, took part in the "Si Tanka Wokiksuye," or Big Foot Memorial Ride. During this spiritual undertaking, on horseback and in wagons, they followed the same trail traveled by Big Foot and his followers from the Cheyenne River to Wounded Knee. One participant, Arthur Zimiga of Pine Ridge Reservation, stated that enduring wind chills as great as 60 below zero made the memorial riders of 1990 feel more solidarity with their 1890 predecessors. A special ceremony was held at the massacre site on the 29th. More than 2,000 people attended the subsequent memorial pow-wow in Kyle, South Dakota. A center for Wounded Knee memorial projects and for the continuing collection of historical information on the tragedy is Oglala Lakota College, Kyle, South Dakota 57752.

Special notice is taken of the remarkable memorial exhibition, *Wounded Knee: Lest We Forget.* This 1990-1991 presentation of museum items relevant to the Ghost Dance and Wounded Knee was sponsored by the Buffalo Bill Historical Center, Cody, Wyoming. Its organizer was George P. Horse Capture, Curator of the Plains Indian Museum. Public showings of the exhibition were from September 17 through November 30, 1990, in Cody; and December 15 through March 15, 1991, in Pierre, South Dakota. The exhibition is described in Josephy, Thomas, and Eder (1990).

THE FUTURE

The Lakota people still experience the hurt, sorrow, and defeat shared by most Native Americans. However, many have seen the 100th anniversary of Wounded Knee as a chance to begin something deeply worthwhile...mending their sacred hoop – the Lakota nation's traditional perception of identity, unity, and being in the integrated universe. Arthur Zimiga expressed to the author, early in 1991, his ardent hope that this renewed sense of meaning among the Lakota will continue. I share that hope.